SONG FOR JIMI

THE STORY OF GUITAR LEGEND JIMI HENDRIX

CHARLES R. SMITH JR.
EDEL RODRIGUEZ

NEAL PORTER BOOKS

HOLIDAY HOUSE / NEW YORK

Neal Porter Books

HOLIDAY HOUSE is registered in the U.S. Patent and Trademark Office.
Printed and bound in May 2021 at C & C Offset, Shenzhen, China.
The artwork for this book was created with oil-based woodblock ink on paper, combined with digital media.
www.holidayhouse.com
First Edition
1   3   5   7   9   10   8   6   4   2

Library of Congress Cataloging-in-Publication Data

Names: Smith, Charles R., Jr., 1969– author. | Rodriguez, Edel,
illustrator.
Title: Song for Jimi / by Charles Smith ; illustrated by Edel Rodriguez.
Description: First edition. | New York City : Holiday House, 2021.
Includes bibliographical references. | Audience: Ages 7 + | Audience:
Grades 2–3 | Summary: "The story of guitarist Jimi Hendrix's career told
in verse"— Provided by publisher.
Identifiers: LCCN 2020044121 | ISBN 9780823443338 (hardcover)
Subjects: LCSH: Hendrix, Jimi—Juvenile literature. | Guitarists—United
States—Biography—Juvenile literature. | Rock musicans—United
States—Biography—Juvenile literature.
Classification: LCC ML3930.H45 S73 2021 | DDC 787.87166092 [B]—dc23
LC record available at https://lccn.loc.gov/2020044121

ISBN 978-0-8234-4333-8 (hardcover)

*Dedicated to all the outcasts, misfits, and unique individuals
who, like Jimi, want to wave their freak flag high. —C.R.S.*

For Gabrielle and Sofia —E.R.

VERSE 1

Jimmy's Blues

Let me tell you a story,
a story 'bout a boy
who became a man,
a git-tar man,
named Jimi.

Now,
with his magic left hand
this git-tar man
could strum silver strings
and conjure a rainbow of sound
that screeched past the stars,
echoed off the moon,
and earthquaked planet Mars.

WRRRRRRIIIIINNNNNNNN
YEAHHHH,
Jimi was far out!

But dig,
Jimi wasn't born
with that magic left hand,
so let's rewind in time
to when his life began.

Let's rewind back
to 1942, November 27,
when Jimi Hendrix was born
as baby Johnny Allen.

That's right, Johnny Allen.
But in three years he became
James Marshall when Daddy
changed his boy's name—
the first change of many—
and soon after that
everyone called him Jimmy.

Now, Jimmy kept to himself,
no, he didn't much speak.
Some thought he was deaf,
the boy acted so meek.

But Jimmy could hear,
oh yeah, that's right,
he could hear Mama and Daddy
drink and fight,
and it scared the voice right out of him
to hear
SCREAMing
every night.

So Jimmy would hide,
hide in the closet,
scared and alone,
trying to keep quiet.

See, Lucille and Al
were a hard-fightin' mix,
breakin' up and makin' up
'til finally they split.
See, Lucille needed to be free,
so she left, she just split.

And Jimmy, well, he missed his mama,
so that boy began to cry.
I say he missed his mama so much
all he could do was ask, *Why?*

Why you leavvvvvvve me, Mama?
Mama, why did you go?

Don't you love your sweet baby?
Mama, don't you love me so?

So Jimmy lived the blues,
oh yeah, Jimmy lived the blues,
from his tattered family tree
to his cardboard-soled shoes.

But buried deep
beneath his beat-up family tree
were roots made strong
by the blood of Cherokee,
warrior roots from his grandmother
that gave Jimmy strength.

So Jimmy taught himself to draw
what his words couldn't say,
and each picture that boy drew
blew his blues away.

But Jimmy's imagination
really began to bloom
when he listened to the radio
and strummed along with his broom.

Elvis,
Little Richard,
Muddy Waters,
and Buddy Holly.
B.B. King,
John Lee Hooker,
and Big Bill Broonzy.
All filled Jimmy's ears
with their git-tar sound.
A sound so sweet
that soon Jimmy found
his fingers pluck-plucking
every day and every night
with that broom,
with that broom,
and soon
Jimmy began to dream
his broom was a git-tar,
then Jimmy began to dream
he was a git-tar superstar.

But dig,
Jimmy's rainbow-colored dreams
were clouded by blue reality.
A reality with his mama
running 'round in the streets,
a reality where his daddy
had trouble making ends meet,
a reality where Jimmy
didn't always eat
and the Hendrix family
didn't always have heat.

Now, about this time
Jimmy was fourteen years old,
and music, sweet music,
began to take hold.

Jimmy graduated from the broom
to a one-string ukulele
to a worn-out, beat-up
acoustic he played daily,
and even though that git-tar
had frayed strings,
Jimmy *plinked*
and Jimmy *plunked*
until those frayed strings could sing.

Now, Jimmy was born lefty
but his daddy Al believed
the left hand was of the devil,
so Jimmy learned to deceive
his daddy when he practiced
by playing with his right hand,
and before Jimmy knew it
he could play with either hand.
That's right, that boy could play his
git-tar with his left and right hand.

But at the age of fifteen,
Jimmy's eyes opened wide
when he learned that his mama,
Lucille, had died.

Yeah, Lucille died
and Jimmy cried,
Jimmy cried.
Jimmy's wide-eyes dripped tears
like the gray Seattle sky.

And oh how Jimmy's tears
did flow,
did flow
for Lucille,
his mama,
'cause Jimmy loved his mama so.
But when his daddy said no
and wouldn't let Jimmy go
see his mama off to heaven
it pained Jimmy so,
I say it broke his heart so.

But all that hurt
and all that pain
and all those tears
that flowed like rain
became
sounds for Jimmy,
trapped in his head,
sounds *EXPLODING*
in fire-bright red,
sounds that could *ECHO*
to the farthest star,
sounds he could unleash
with a git-tar.

VERSE 2

Red Hands

Plink plink plink
Jimmy *plinked* that one string
until his world changed
one day at sixteen.
Jimmy's first guitar!
Jimmy's first real guitar!
A white Supro Ozark electric guitar!

That's right, a git-tar
given to him by Daddy.
His very own git-tar,
and it made Jimmy happy,
like Christmas-morning-
times-five kind of happy.

And that git-tar became
a voice for Jimmy's soul,
and that git-tar made
Jimmy's broken life whole.

Now, Jimmy needed
to play in a band,
he needed to hear sound
coming from his hand,
he needed to hear sound
amplified *LOUD*,
but first he needed an amp
to play in front of a crowd.

So Jimmy joined a band
called the Rocking Kings,
and they had an amp
so Jimmy could do his thing.

Now, Jimmy was in ninth grade
but school *wasn't* his thing.
See, he got an F in music
'cause school just wasn't his scene,
and his music teacher said he should
give up the guitar thing.
That's right, his teacher said he should
give up on his dream.

But Jimmy practiced hard
and Jimmy practiced long,
and every day Jimmy
learned a new song.
That's right, every day he
learned a new song.

Jimmy's sound was raw,
VRENNNNNNNN
and Jimmy's sound was wild,
VRENN ROWNNN RREEEEE
but Jimmy was determined
to find his own style.
So Jimmy became
a musical sponge,
absorbing a little
something from everyone.

From sax players he learned
to swoop and soar
over the rhythm section
to move feet on the dance floor.

From bluesmen he studied
their show-stopping tricks,
like playing behind his back with
lightning-quick flicks.

And so, when Jimmy played
to small, assorted crowds,
he imitated his idols
by playing hard and loud,
ROWNN-ROWNNN ROWN-ROWN-ROWNNN ROWNNNNNN YEAH!
He imitated his idols
by playing with lots of flash,
causing Jimmy and his own
bandmates to clash.

Then Jimmy began
to steal the spotlight,
taking solos and plucking
like a wild man every night.
With feathers on his git-tar,
you know, Jimmy was quite a sight.

*Who is this cat
playing with his left hand?*
everyone asked
when Jimmy took the stand.
But at the end of each set
they all knew Jimmy's name,
they all knew his left hand
could flicker like a flame.

Now, ever since he was a child
Jimmy moved quite a bit
and never settled into school life
so at seventeen he quit.
That's right, to play music
Jimmy dropped out
and quit.

Jimmy had his git-tar
and he knew how to use it,
even though Al fought with him
for playing *the devil's music*.

But that music was coming
from a fire inside,
raging in Jimmy,
he just couldn't hide.
That music was coming
from soul-scorching *SCREAMS*
from Mama and Daddy
that haunted Jimmy's dreams.

So when Jimmy turned eighteen
he wanted to be free
from Al's rules and abuse and
general tyranny.

But options for a dropout
proved not to be
many, so Jimmy
joined the army.
That's right, like his daddy,
Jimmy joined the army.

A Screaming Eagle paratrooper
Jimmy wanted to be,
but what Jimmy wanted most
was to simply be free.

VERSE 3
Sunshine Yellow

Eighteen, in the army,
miles from home,
Jimmy was free
and finally on his own.

Basic training in California,
then off to become
a Screaming Eagle in Kentucky
where he would learn to jump from
planes that pierced clouds
in the ocean-blue sky,
high in the heavens
where Jimmy could *FLY*.

The *ROAAAARRRR* of the plane
and *SSSHHHHHHH* of the wind
filled Jimmy's eardrums
with inspiration.

Back on the ground
Jimmy searched for that sound,
Jimmy picked at his git-tar
for that plane-rattlin' sound.

Soon, Jimmy became known
as the "guitar-playing freak,"
and his bunkmates began
to taunt and tweak
and tease and test
and steal and hide
Jimmy's git-tar
for some peace and quiet.

See, every night Jimmy
went to sleep in his bed
with his git-tar, and plucked
the sounds in his head.

The *SCREEEEAMS*
the *SMACKS*
the *WHIRRRRS*
the *CRACCCKKKS*
the *ROARRRRS*
the *SHHHHHSSS*
the *THWIPPPS*
the *THWACKS*
and *SHRIEKS*
all creeped
into Jimmy's hand
while Jimmy was asleep.

And all those sounds
filled Jimmy's dreams
as he played them onstage
to shrieks and screams.

But reality hit Jimmy
smack in the face:
every morning he woke up
to the military pace.

*Line up
push-up
march
shut up.*

And Jimmy grew tired,
tired of conforming;
he wanted to be free,
on stage, performing.

Free
as the yellow
sun shining in the sky,
Jimmy wanted to be free
and was ready to fly.

So Jimmy flew the coop
and got discharged early,
leaving behind
the cage of the army.

But while on base
Jimmy had a buddy who
played with him in a band, and
soon he was out too.

So together the two
musicians moved to
Nashville, Tennessee,
to see what they could do.

Now, Nashville was a hot
music-making spot
but the music was divided
by color,
so Jimmy got
a firsthand education
in music segregation
down south,
and it gave Jimmy
a new motivation.

Now, Jimmy could play,
oh yeah, Jimmy could play,
but when he asked the old bluesmen
for advice they would say:

Slow down, boy,
slow that hand down.
Use them long fingers of yours
to shape your own sound.

See what you need
is some mud on your boots
and a little mo' control.
To play them blues, boy,
you gotta play from yo' soul.

To play them blues, see,
you gotta walk that walk.
I say to play them blues,
you gotta make that git-tar talk.

So Jimmy hit the road,
git-tar in hand,
traveling band to band
across the land.

Over through Virginia,
down to Texas and Florida,
back to Tennessee,
to Kentucky and Indiana.
Arkansas, Kansas City,
Missouri, and Atlanta,
Georgia, with his git-tar
Jimmy learned lots of tricks,
like playing blindfolded,
teeth-scratching licks.

Jimmy used his long fingers
to hold high notes so sweet,
and Jimmy's git-tar spoke
like a bird learning to tweet.

And when that bird returned home
to his nest in Tennessee,
Jimmy spread his wings again
and flew off to NYC.

VERSE 4.
Peacock with a Pick

With blues in his heart,
fire in his hand,
and mud on his boots,
Jimmy stood as a man.

Age twenty-one,
free as can be,
a mannish boy
in Harlem, NYC.

But in Harlem, Jimmy
was a curiosity,
a wild-haired peacock
bopping to his own beat.

See, Jimmy hummed to himself,
walking down the street,
and with that git-tar on his back
he was laughed at endlessly.

But word got around
that the peacock could play,
and band leaders invited Jimmy
to play for a little pay.

Now, Jimmy tried hard
to play as he was told,
but with one pluck,
VRRRRRRNNNNNN
out of control.

LOUD
TWEAKING
TWONKING
ROARRRRRIIINNGGG!

Jimmy took off
on a solo, soaring,
floating, flying
like an eagle in the sky,
spreading his wings
beneath the yellow sun high.

Flying solo
for oh so long,
band leaders fired Jimmy
on the spot: *So long!*

And it wasn't long before Jimmy
said *So long*
to bands uptown.

So he swooped downtown.

Down to the Village
to spread wide his wings,
and ears popped open
when Jimmy did his thing.

Playing that git-tar
on stage with his teeth,
Jimmy amplified his arrival
loud as can be.

And once again word
soon got around,
that this peacock downtown
was plucking a new sound,
plucking an odd sound,
plucking a rock-folk, rhythm-and-blues sound.

But even though Jimmy's sound
was the talk of downtown,
sometimes Jimmy found
himself sleeping on the ground.

That's right, Jimmy found
himself sleeping under the stars,
flat broke, belly empty,
just him and his git-tar.

But Jimmy kept working,
working that left hand,
and began to write songs
'cause he wanted his own band.

Yeah, Jimmy scribbled
of angels and planet Mars,
grandma's Cherokee stories,
and childhood scars.

But when Jimmy was little
he st-st-stuttered,
a habit he developed
from losing his mother.

So when memories of Mama
flash-backed bright as day,
his git-tar *SCREAMED*
what Jimmy couldn't say.

MAMAWHYYYYYYY
WHHHYYYYY MAMAWHHHYYYYYY
MAMA-MAMAWHYYYYY
MAMAWHYYYYYEEEYYYYYY

But to lead his own band
Jimmy would *have* to sing,
so speaking words, not singing words,
became Jimmy's thing.

And soon Jimmy changed
his name to Jimmy James
and Jimmy James formed
a band called the Blue Flames.

Now, the Blue Flames played
mostly the blues,
but under Jimmy's hand
even the blues changed hues.

And under Jimmy's hand
even short radio hits
became sonic epics
when Jimmy twisted riffs.

Then a friendship began
and blossomed with a fan,
and that fan knew folks
that could give Jimmy a hand.

But to those folks, Jimmy
was way too raw,
until a pair of *eyes*
couldn't believe what they saw.

On stage stood a peacock
speaking through his git-tar,
and a pair of *ears* knew
that peacock could be a star.

Those eyes and those ears
happened to belong
to a big producer looking
to make a hit song.

He already had the song
but needed a musician,
and there before his eyes
stood a git-tar magician,
a sonic tactician,
a Picasso with a pick
painting in the blues tradition.

So he invited Jimmy
to London to record,
and with no cage to hold him
Jimmy flew across the shore.

On the plane Jimmy James
became Jimi, with an *i*,
a more exotic Jimi,
one *m*, no *y*.

From the moment Jimi landed
he was introduced around
as the next big thing
the big producer had found.

Now, this producer knew
all the English git-tar greats
and he couldn't wait to showcase
his import from the States.

When Jimi took the stage,
wild hair and black skin,
Jimi's git-tar spoke
of all the places he had been.

Childhood sighs
beneath gray Seattle skies
became silver jet engines
piercing blue skies.

A slow, Southern drawl
filled with New York City style
echoed into ears
as Jimi played out each mile.

And when all those git-tar greats
heard Jimi Hendrix play,
they wanted to quit playing
'cause Jimi blew them all away.

Yeah, those git-tar gods
all bowed to Jimi's hand,
so now the big producer
needed a band for that hand.

The first man in Jimi's band
was the bass player,
a white cat from England
with afro-puffed hair.

Last was a drummer,
making the trio complete,
a white jazz cat
who banged a driving beat.

Now these two English cats
knew how to play,
but playing behind Jimi,
they kept out of the way.

Because watching Jimi play
was a full-body experience,
so when the band needed a name
they became
THE JIMI HENDRIX EXPERIENCE.

Soon Jimi and his band
began to tour the land:
cities across England,
Germany, and France.

Too weird for back home,
Jimi found freedom in England,
and legend of his git-tar
grew everywhere Jimi plugged in.

As the Experience would play
Jimi experimented with sound,
making his git-tar *FEEEEEEEEED*back,
like metal scraping the ground.

Eyes popped, jaws dropped
and ears almost bled
when Jimi plucked the fireworks
exploding in his head.

Tangerine *SCREAMS*
screeched through loud,
yellow sun*BURSTS*,
electrifying the crowd.

Now, as loud as Jimi's git-tar was
his voice was just as quiet,
and even though Jimi hated to sing
the producer convinced him to try it.

So, for the first time Jimi sang his words
and the band recorded a hit;
next up was an album
filled with Jimi's own lyrics.

Looking back on life,
Jimi began to write
stories of peace,
stories of strife,
memories of heartbreak,
memories of love,
dreams of angels
in the heavens above,
warrior stories
of Cherokee ancestry,
lovesick blues,
science-fiction and fantasy,
heartfelt lines
about happy times,
blues-filled lines
about ugly times,
no food, no shelter,
without-a-dime kinds of times.

Yeah, Jimi lived those lines
that filled song lyric rhymes,
but Jimi's git-tar was the star
that made his words shine.

Fast, slow,
heavy or light,
Jimi's range on the git-tar
made Jimi shine bright.

But dig, back home in America
no one knew Jimi's name,
but once the album came out
that would soon change.

See, Jimi received
a life-changing invite
that involved a music festival
and an overseas flight.

The three-day festival
needed a showstopping finish,
so one of the Beatles recommended
the Jimi Hendrix Experience.

Yeah, Jimi stood as a groovy
genius of the strings,
just ten years removed
from his broom at age fourteen.

Now, age twenty-four,
Jimi's star would shoot higher
when he touched down in California
to set America on fire.

OUTRO
Song for Jimi

June 18, 1967
MONTEREY POP FESTIVAL
Monterey, California

Peacock *louuuuud*,
black and *prouuuuud*
standing *ouuuuut*
from the *crowwwwwwd*,
Jimi flicks his fingers
over
silver *striiiiings*
then
hits a high note
'til it *SCREAMMMMMMMS*
LOOK OUT!

No one
before you
ever did what you do,
the way that you do that
groovy git-tar voo-doo.

Jimi,
no one
before you
could play the style
that you do
when you unleash that
funky-freaky-groovy
git-tar voo-doo
HEYYY!

INTERLUDE

Now lemme break it down. . . .

Dig,
Jimi was a wild thing
on the git-tar strings,
and those folks in Monterey
never heard such a display
when Jimi fried their ears
with his white-hot git-tar play.
But Jimi wasn't done,
oh no, he wasn't done.
The crowd had no idea
of what was to come.
Yeah, Jimi pulled out
all his show-stopping tricks,
you know, behind-the-back, between-the-legs,
teeth-plucking licks.

But Jimi topped himself
when he dropped to the ground
and *KNOCKED* notes on his git-tar,
then held onto the sound,
gave his git-tar one last kiss
and with a quick match strike
Jimi set his git-tar on fire
with flames flickering bright.
Then Jimi *SMASHED* that git-tar
as tribal drums kept beating
and Jimi's git-tar held that high note,
amplified and screeching
like a Cherokee warrior
screeching a fierce battle cry,
as Jimi showed the world
how to kiss the sky.
YEAHH!

A NOTE FROM THE AUTHOR

I don't remember when I was first introduced to the music of Jimi Hendrix, but I do remember when I fell in love with it. I was eighteen, the youngest and only Black student of about 750 at a small photography school. When I started classes I felt isolated and alone. Eventually I made some friends and bonded with them over a love of music. We introduced each other to our favorites, and when someone played Jimi Hendrix, I didn't know who it was. Sure, I had heard his music before, but I was only familiar with a few songs. As I began hearing more, I remember telling my mother I was getting into him, and she said she never liked Jimi because he was too loud.

But that was exactly why I liked him. He was soft-spoken but played loud. He was colorful. And since he was a different type of Black artist, he was often teased by the Black community. I identified with that. I wasn't loud, but I was also teased for being different. Books and words were to me what music was to Jimi. That can make you an outcast amongst your own people. Listening to his music I could feel his pain, his wild creativity, and his mastery of the guitar that allowed him to play with great freedom. I listened to everything I could find and wanted to learn more about the man behind the music.

Back then there was no Google, so I went to bookstores and libraries to learn more about Jimi. I learned that he died too young, left behind a handful of albums, and was respected by the most gifted guitarists. I didn't learn much more about him, so I just continued enjoying his music over the years. In 2008, while visiting Cleveland, Ohio, I had a chance to tour the Rock & Roll Hall of Fame, where Jimi had his own section. Of all the unique items on display, what caught my eye were some crayon drawings that he made when he was a child. I don't recall reading anything about his childhood or teen years; most of what I found centered around his music and his death. That immediately got my wheels spinning. I wanted to tell his childhood story. I wanted to show how that young boy went on to become one of the greatest guitarists of all time.

Since Jimi was a musician, I decided to use a song structure and break the book into verses. Jimi merged a variety of styles to create his own, so each verse is reflective of a different style. The book starts with his difficult childhood and moves at a slow pace, like his blues songs. To describe the sounds he made, I watched films of his live shows and tried to put down on paper what I saw and heard. The last verse of the book, "Outro: Song for Jimi," takes its rhythm from one of his most popular songs, "Crosstown Traffic."

As I approached the ending, I knew I didn't want to finish with his death; Jimi died tragically at the age of twenty-seven, presumably of drug- and alcohol-related causes. Instead, I wanted to end with a moment of triumph. I wanted to celebrate a unique individual who inspired me. I wanted to show how he became the legend we know today. Jimi Hendrix may no longer be with us, but he lives on through his music.

—Charles R. Smith

TIMELINE

1942 On November 27, Jimi is born Johnny Allen Hendrix in Seattle, Washington. His parents, Al and Lucille, are dancers. Three years later, Al changes Johnny's name to James Marshall Hendrix.

1953 Jimi begins following the pop charts and listening to radio. Pretends to play along, strumming a broom as if it were a guitar.

1955 Introduced to blues music by neighbors.

1956 Graduates from broom to a one-string ukulele found by his father.

1958 Begins to play a secondhand acoustic guitar purchased by his father for five dollars.

Receives an F in music class.

Forms his first group, the Velvetones, but quits after only three months.

During the summer Al buys  Jimi his first electric guitar, a white Supro Ozark 1560S. Jimi begins learning a new song every day.

1959 Joins another group, the Rocking Kings.

1961 –62 Serves in the US Army, trains as a paratrooper, and earns the Screaming Eagle patch of the 101st Airborne Division.

While in the army, Jimi meets bass player Billy Cox and the two begin to jam. They find a drummer and form a band, the King Kasuals.

After multiple disciplinary complaints, Jimi is granted a general discharge under honorable conditions barely a year after enlisting.

1962 Relocates to Clarksville, Tennessee. The King Kasuals start out playing local gigs before moving to Nashville, where they become the house band for a local club.

1963 Jimi travels around the South, performing at a variety of venues. Begins working as a backup musician for blues and R&B artists such as Sam Cooke and B.B. King.

1964 Leaves Nashville and moves to Harlem, in New York City. In February, enters an amateur contest at the Apollo Theater, winning first place and a twenty-five dollar prize. Starts playing the Harlem club circuit as a "sideman"—a guitarist for hire—for R&B groups such as the Isley Brothers.

1965 Plays his first televised performance with Little Richard's band. Later that year, meets Curtis Knight in the lobby of a hotel and joins his band, Curtis Knight and the Squires.

1966 Frustrated as a sideman "playing the same notes and the same beat" with R&B groups in Harlem, Jimi begins playing folk and alternative venues in Greenwich Village. He starts the band Jimmy James and the Blue Flames and is able to play as a lead guitarist for the first time.

On July 5, Chas Chandler, former bassist for the Animals, hears Jimi at the Cafe Wha? and eventually becomes his manager.

On September 23, Jimi flies to London, England, with Chandler. The producer convinces "Jimmy James" to revert to his original last name and modify his first name to "Jimi."

He then forms the band the Jimi Hendrix Experience with drummer Mitch Mitchell and bass player Noel Redding. They tour France immediately.

In December, "Hey Joe" debuts in the UK, peaking at No. 6 on the singles chart.

1967 While on a tour of the UK, Jimi sets his guitar on fire for the first time during a show at the Finsbury Park Astoria in London.

The band's first album, *Are You Experienced*, is released in the UK on May 12 and in the US on August 23.

On June 18, the Jimi Hendrix Experience performs at the Monterey Pop Festival. The recognition they receive from Jimi's performance catapults them into fame in the US.

Their second studio album, *Axis: Bold as Love*, is released in the UK on December 1 and in the US the next month, on January 15.

Around this time, Jimi begins to take a more active role in the direction and mixing of each track.

1968 In October a third studio album is released, an ambitious double album titled *Electric Ladyland*, produced by Chas Chandler and Jimi Hendrix. Jimi begins work on his own recording studio, Electric Lady Studios.

1969 The Jimi Hendrix Experience breaks up due to the pressure of touring and friction during recording sessions. Jimi begins working with other musicians, eventually forming the Band of Gypsys with Billy Cox and Buddy Miles.

On August 18, Jimi performs at the Woodstock Festival. His rendition of "The Star-Spangled Banner" is the highlight of the festival and becomes a legendary moment in rock history.

1970 In April, *Band of Gypsys*, an album compiled from four live performances, is released in the US.

On September 18, Jimi is found unresponsive in a London apartment and pronounced dead.

1992 The Jimi Hendrix Experience is inducted into the Rock & Roll Hall of Fame.

PERSONAL PLAYLIST

Even though Jimi made only three studio albums and one live album during his lifetime, he recorded plenty of music. Rather than just list all of his songs and posthumous recordings, I've created a playlist of the ones that inspired me throughout the writing of this book.

From *Are You Experienced*
"Hey Joe," written by Billy Roberts
"Purple Haze"
"I Don't Live Today"
"The Wind Cries Mary"

From *Axis: Bold as Love*
"Spanish Castle Magic"
"Castles Made of Sand"

From *Electric Ladyland*
"Voodoo Child (Slight Return)"
"Crosstown Traffic"
"Gypsy Eyes"
"All Along the Watchtower," written by Bob Dylan

From *Jimi Hendrix: Live at Woodstock*, MCA Records MCAD2-11987, 1999
"Star Spangled Banner"

DISCOGRAPHY

Studio Albums

Are You Experienced. Reprise Records RS 6261, 1967
Axis: Bold as Love. Reprise Records RS 6281, 1968
Electric Ladyland. Reprise Records 2RS 6307, 1968

Live Album

Band of Gypsys. Capitol Records STAO-472, 1970

A partial list of the many recordings and videos that have been released following Jimi's death can be found here: jimihendrix.com/music.

REFERENCES

Cross, Charles R. *Room Full of Mirrors: A Biography of Jimi Hendrix.* New York: Hachette, 2005.

Henderson, David. *'Scuse Me While I Kiss the Sky: Jimi Hendrix: Voodoo Child.* New York: Atria Books, 2008.

Hendrix, Janie L., and John McDermott. *Jimi Hendrix: An Illustrated Experience.* New York: Atria Books, 2007.

Lawrence, Sharon. *Jimi Hendrix: The Intimate Story of a Betrayed Musical Legend.* New York: It Books/HarperCollins, 2006.

Shapiro, Harry, and Caesar Glebbeek. *Jimi Hendrix: Electric Gypsy.* New York: St. Martin's Griffin, 1995.

The Jimi Hendrix Experience: Live at Monterey. Universal Music, 2007, DVD.

www.jimihendrix.com